LETTERS OF NOTE: GRIEF

Letters of Note was born in 2009 with the launch of lettersofnote.com, a website celebrating old-fashioned correspondence that has since been visited over 100 million times. The first *Letters of Note* volume was published in October 2013, followed later that year by the first Letters Live, an event at which world-class performers delivered remarkable letters to a live audience.

Since then, these two siblings have grown side by side, with *Letters of Note* becoming an international phenomenon, and Letters Live shows being staged at iconic venues around the world, from London's Royal Albert Hall to the theatre at the Ace Hotel in Los Angeles.

You can find out more at lettersofnote.com and letterslive.com. And now you can also listen to the audio editions of the new series of *Letters of Note*, read by an extraordinary cast drawn from the wealth of talent that regularly takes part in the acclaimed Letters Live shows.

Letters of Note

GRIEF

COMPILED BY

Shaun Usher

PENGUIN BOOKS

For all who have lost

PENGUIN BOOKS
An imprint of Penguin Random House LLC
penguinrandomhouse.com

First published in Great Britain by Canongate Books Ltd 2021
Published in Penguin Books 2022

Library of Congress Cataloging-in-Publication Data
Names: Usher, Shaun, compiler.
Title: Letters of note. Grief / compiled by Shaun Usher.
Other titles: Grief
Description: [New York] : Penguin Books, 2022. |
Series: Letters of note ; 8
Identifiers: LCCN 2021025586 (print) |
LCCN 2021025587 (ebook) |
ISBN 9780143136781 (trade paperback) |
ISBN 9780525508281 (ebook)
Subjects: LCSH: Bereaved persons—Correspondence. |
Grief. Classification: LCC BF575.G7 L483 2022 (print) |
LCC BF575.G7 (ebook) |
DDC 152.4—dc23
LC record available at https://lccn.loc.gov/2021025586
LC ebook record available at https://lccn.loc.gov/2021025587

Printed in the United States of America
1st Printing

Set in Joanna MT.

CONTENTS

A letter is a time bomb, a message in a bottle, a spell, a cry for help, a story, an expression of concern, a ladle of love, a way to connect through words. This simple and brilliantly democratic art form remains a potent means of communication and, regardless of whatever technological revolution we are in the middle of, the letter lives and, like literature, it always will.

INTRODUCTION

The book you now hold is a carefully curated collection of thirty-one letters, the earliest written in 45 BC, the most recent in 2019, from the pens and typewriters of novelists, spiritual leaders, activists, musicians, politicians, poets and everyday folk, sent from addresses in all corners of the globe.

Tying them all together is grief, an emotional process we are all destined to experience as we stumble blindly through life – for grief is our natural reaction to loss. It is the pit that forms in our stomach as a loved one walks away, or the paralysing wave of darkness that arrives just as someone dies. Grief can cause pain and tears, bring strange consolation or overwhelm. It can sometimes do all at once. We can grieve the loss of anyone or anything, be it a person, an animal, a job or a dream, and it is important to remind ourselves that there is no correct way to do so, for although grief is universal, it manifests differently for all. By its very nature, the grieving process is often lonely. Some people grieve in silence, either through choice or circumstance; others need to find a way to put their grief into words, to make sense somehow of the experience and translate it into a recognisable form. Maybe, just maybe, if it can be articulated, it can help us, in some way.

Over the years I have compiled many different collections of letters, on subjects ranging from Love to Art, from Music to Sex, from War to Dogs. It is no exaggeration to say that researching this particular volume, Grief, has been, all at once, the most heartbreaking, enlightening, fulfilling and rewarding of them all. To be able to read the words of those who have lost so much, and the words of those attempting to console, even a little, those who are grieving is something of an honour.

It is my hope that Letters of Note: Grief may act as another tool with which those of you who are suffering loss can ease your pain, by reminding you that you are not alone in your suffering, that there have been others out there and will be others again. Similar paths have been walked.

Shaun Usher
2020

The Letters

LETTER 01
SORROW MUST BE SORROW
George Eliot to Lady Lytton
8 July 1870

To most people, Mary Ann Evans is better known as George Eliot, a pen name which adorns the covers of her seven novels – including, most notably, Middlemarch, A Study of Provincial Life, which is considered to be her masterpiece. It was in July of 1870, a year before that novel's publication, that Eliot wrote this letter. Her friend, Lady Lytton, was dealing with the recent loss of her uncle, George Villiers, 4th Earl of Clarendon, who for all intents and purposes had for many years acted as her father.

THE LETTER

I did not like to write to you until Mr. Lytton sent
word that I might do so, because I had not the
intimate knowledge that would have enabled me to
measure your trouble; and one dreads, of all things,
to speak or write a wrong or unseasonable word
when words are the only signs of interest and
sympathy that one has to give. I know now, from
what your dear husband has told us, that your loss
is very keenly felt by you, that it has first made you
acquainted with acute grief, and this makes me
think of you very much. For learning to love any
one is like an increase of property—it increases
care, and brings many new fears lest precious
things should come to harm. I find myself often
thinking of you with that sort of proprietor's
anxiety, wanting you to have gentle weather all
through your life, so that your face may never look
worn and storm-beaten, and wanting your husband
to be and do the very best, lest anything short of
that should be disappointment to you. At present
the thought of you is all the more with me because
your trouble has been brought by death; and for
nearly a year death seems to me my most intimate

3

daily companion. I mingle the thought of it with every other, not sadly, but as one mingles the thought of some one who is nearest in love and duty with all one's motives. I try to delight in the sunshine that will be when I shall never see it any more. And I think it is possible for this sort of impersonal life to attain great intensity—possible for us to gain much more independence than is usually believed of the small bundle of facts that make our own personality. I don't know why I should say this to you, except that my pen is chatting as my tongue would if you were here. We women are always in danger of living too exclusively in the affections, and though our affections are, perhaps, the best gifts we have, we ought also to have our share of the more independent life—some joy in things for their own sake. It is piteous to see the helplessness of some sweet women when their affections are disappointed; because all their teaching has been that they can only delight in study of any kind for the sake of a personal love. They have never contemplated an independent delight in ideas as an experience which they could confess without being laughed at. Yet surely women need this sort of defence against passionate affliction even more than men. Just under the pressure of grief, I do not believe there is any consolation. The word seems to me to be drapery for falsities. Sorrow must be sorrow, ill must be ill, till duty and love towards all who remain recover their rightful predominance. Your life is so full of those claims that you will not have time for brooding over the unchangeable. Do not spend any of your valuable time now in writing to me, but be satisfied with sending me news of you through Mr. Lytton when he has occasion to write to Mr. Lewes.

I have lately finished reading aloud Mendelssohn's "Letters", which we had often resolved and failed to read before. They have been quite cheering to us from the sense they give of communion with an eminently pure, refined nature, with the most rigorous conscience in art. In the evening we have always a concert to listen to—a concert of modest pretensions, but well conducted enough to be agreeable.

I hope this letter of chit-chat will not reach you at a wrong moment. In any case, forgive all mistakes on the part of one who is always yours sincerely and affectionately.

LETTER 02
GRIEF IS NON-NEGOTIABLE
Nick Cave – Letter to Cynthia
The Red Hand Files, October 2018

Nick Cave was born in 1957 in the Australian town of Warracknabeal, to Dawn and Colin Cave. The formation of his first band at Caulfield Grammar School in a suburb of Melbourne ignited a decades-long career. Over the years, he has produced acclaimed music, both as a solo artist and with his band, Nick Cave & the Bad Seeds, acted on stage and screen, and written film scores and screenplays. Throughout, Cave has taken time to connect with his fans, and in 2018 he launched 'The Red Hand Files', an online platform through which they are able to ask questions of him directly, his answers published for all to see. In 2018, a letter arrived from someone named Cynthia, which read:

> *I have experienced the death of my father, my sister, and my first love in the past few years and feel that I have some communication with them, mostly through dreams. They are helping me. Are you and Susie feeling that your son Arthur is with you and communicating in some way?*

Arthur was Nick Cave's late son. He died in 2015 aged fifteen.
This letter was Cave's reply.

THE LETTER

Dear Cynthia,

This is a very beautiful question and I am grateful
that you have asked it. It seems to me, that if we
love, we grieve. That's the deal. That's the pact. Grief
and love are forever intertwined. Grief is the
terrible reminder of the depths of our love and,
like love, grief is non-negotiable. There is a vastness
to grief that overwhelms our minuscule selves. We
are tiny, trembling clusters of atoms subsumed
within grief's awesome presence. It occupies the
core of our being and extends through our fingers
to the limits of the universe. Within that whirling
gyre all manner of madnesses exist: ghosts and
spirits and dream visitations, and everything else
that we, in our anguish, will into existence. These
are precious gifts that are as valid and as real as we
need them to be. They are the spirit guides that
lead us out of the darkness.

I feel the presence of my son, all around, but he
may not be there. I hear him talk to me, parent me,
guide me, though he may not be there. He visits
Susie in her sleep regularly, speaks to her, comforts
her, but he may not be there. Dread grief trails
bright phantoms in its wake. These spirits are ideas,
essentially. They are our stunned imaginations

reawakening after the calamity. Like ideas, these spirits speak of possibility. Follow your ideas, because on the other side of the idea is change and growth and redemption. Create your spirits. Call to them. Will them alive. Speak to them. It is their impossible and ghostly hands that draw us back to the world from which we were jettisoned; better now and unimaginably changed.

With love,

Nick

'IF WE LOVE, WE
GRIEVE, THAT'S THE
DEAL.'

— Nick Cave

A GREAT DESERT LIES AHEAD OF ME

Edith Wharton to John Hugh Smith

15 October 1927

Edith Wharton's lifelong relationship with Walter Van Rensselaer Berry began in 1883, as both holidayed in Bar Harbor, Maine. Their connection was instant and natural. Two years later, she wed another man, Edward, thus beginning an unfulfilling marriage that lasted eighteen years – most of which were unhappy – and ended in divorce. She would later write her most celebrated novel, The Age of Innocence *(1920), for which she was awarded the Pulitzer Prize for Literature: she was, in fact, the first woman to receive the accolade. Six years later, Walter Berry died following a long illness, the final stretch of which saw Wharton take care of him. Shortly after Berry passed away, Wharton wrote this letter to her friend, John Hugh Smith. She would later call Berry 'the great love of all my life'.*

THE LETTER

Pavillon Colombe
St. Brice
October 15, 1927

My dearest John— All my friends have sent me
words of sympathy, but only you have said just
what I wanted, what I needed. Thank you, dear.

Yes, I am glad indeed that it is over, but I
perceive now that I, who thought I loved solitude,
was never for one moment alone—& a great desert
lies ahead of me.

The sense of desolation (though of thankfulness
too, of course) is unspeakably increased by those last
days together, when he wanted me so close, & held
me so fast, that all the old flame & glory came back,
in the cold shadow of death & parting. Oh, my dear,
I sometimes feel I am too old to live through such
hours, & take up the daily round again.

But I remember what you say, & I am proud of
having kept such a perfect friendship after the
great days were over, & always to have felt that,
through all the coming & going of things in his
eager ambitious life, I was there, in the place he
put me in so many years ago, the place of perfect
understanding.

I don't think I ever bothered him but once—& when he felt that the busy brilliant days were over, he liked to have me with him, because he knew I wouldn't fuss & sentimentalize, or try to divert his eyes from the end we both knew they were fixed on. He hated humbug—so do I.—And now I'm so grateful to all my friends for understanding what I feel—& you most, dear John.

Edith

Robert is staying with me, & won't leave till after the funeral. He has been kindness itself.

LETTER 04
I HAVE FELT THIS LOSS WITH ALL MY HEART

Johann Wolfgang von Goethe to Anna Margaretha Textor

February 1771

In 1768, seventy-four-year-old lawyer and then mayor of Frankfurt Johann Wolfgang Textor suffered a stroke from which he would never truly recover. His efforts to continue working proved futile and a year later he withdrew from public office. In February of 1771, he died, leaving behind his wife, Anna, and five children. Shortly after Textor's death, his widow received this letter from one of their grandsons, Johann Wolfgang von Goethe. This was written three years before publication of Goethe's wildly successful debut novel, Die Leiden des jungen Werther (The Sorrows of Young Werther), *which instantly set him on the path to becoming one of the most important figures in the history of literature.*

THE LETTER

Dearest Grandmama,
The death of our dear father, already dreaded from
day to day for so long a time, has yet come upon
me unprepared. I have felt this loss with all my
heart; and what to us is the world around us, when
we lose what we love?

To console myself, and not you, I write to you,
you who are now the head of our family to beg
you for your love, and assure you of my tenderest
devotion. You have lived longer in the world than I,
and must find in your own heart more comfort
than I know of. You have endured more misfortune
than I; you must feel far more vividly than I can
say it that the most sorrowful occurrence often,
through the hand of Providence, takes the most
favorable turn for our happiness; that the succession
of fortune and misfortune in life is intertwined like
sleep and waking, neither without the other, and
one for the sake of the other; that all happiness in
the world is only lent.

You have seen children and grandchildren die
before you, ceasing their work in the morning of

their life; and now your tears accompany a husband to the everlasting Sabbath rest – a man who has honestly earned his wage. He has it now; and yet the good God, whilst he took thought for him has also taken thought for you – for us. He has taken from us not the merry friendly, happy old man who carried on the affairs of the age with the vivacity of a youth, who stood out amongst his fellow-citizens and was the joy of his family. He has now taken from us a man whose life we have seen for some years hanging by a silken thread. His energetic spirit must have felt with painful heaviness the oppressive weight of his sickly body; must have wished himself free, as a prisoner yearns to escape from his cell.

Now he is free, and our tears bid him God-speed; and our sorrow gathers us around you, dear Mama, to console ourselves with you, hearts simply full of love. You have lost much, but much remains to you. Look at us, love us, and be happy. May you enjoy for a long time yet the temporal reward which you have so richly earned of our invalid father, who has gone hence to report it at the place of requital and who has left us behind as tokens of his love, tokens of the past time of sorrowful yet pleasing recollection.

And so may your love for us remain as it was; and where much love is, there is much happiness.

I am, with a truly warm heart, your loving grandchild,

J. W. Goethe

'LOOK AT US, LOVE US,
AND BE HAPPY.'

— J. W. Goethe

LETTER 05
YOUR TRUE SELF HAS NO LIFE, NO DEATH
Sheldon and Seungsahn Haengwon
18 August 1977

Korean Zen master Seungsahn Haengwon was born in 1927 in Suncheon, Pyeongannam-do, North Korea. Aged twenty, fresh from university, he decided to become a Buddhist monk. Decades later, in 1972, having opened temples across Asia, he moved to the United States and founded the Kwan Um School of Zen, a now global network of Zen centres through which his teachings can be learned. Over the years, until his death in 2004, Seungsahn received countless letters from students the world over in which his advice was sought on a range of issues. It is said that he responded personally to each and every one, and that a selection of these letters is read aloud by the centres' Dharma teachers as a way to enlighten their students. This particular exchange occurred in 1977, prompted by the death of a student's father.

THE LETTERS

Dear Soen Sa Nim,

Your letter, newsletter, and picture made me cry—
and I am so grateful. I understand: straightforward
mind, straightforward heart, straightforward speech,
straightforward body.

My father died yesterday. I built a small altar in
my room and sat, and I told him to recognize that
all things are in his own mind—his original
brightness. Too late, I was finally able to say, "I love
you." I am thankful to have your picture on the
altar.

Thank you for your great kindness.

Yours,

Sheldon

*   *   *

August 18, 1977

Dear Sheldon,

Thank you for your letter. How are you?

In your letter, you told me that your father died.
I grieve for you.

Long ago in China when the great Zen Master Nam Cheon died, his students and all those who knew him were very sad. The custom at that time was to go to the dead person's house and cry, "*Aigo! Aigo! Aigo!*" But when the Zen master's best student, a layman named Bu Dae Sa, heard of his teacher's death, he went to Nam Cheon's temple, opened the door, stood in front of the coffin, and laughed, "HA HA HA HA!!"—great laughter.

The many people who were assembled to mourn Nam Cheon's death were surprised at this laughter. The temple Housemaster said, "You were our teacher's best student. Our teacher has died, and everyone is sad. Why are you laughing?"

Bu Dae Sa said, "You say our master has died. Where did he go?" The Housemaster was silent. He could not answer.

Then Bu Dae Sa said, "You don't understand where our teacher went, so I am very sad. *Aigo! Aigo! Aigo!*"

You must understand this. What does this mean? If you have no answer, I grieve for you.

Zen is the great work of life and death. What is life? What is death? When you attain this, then everything is clear, everything is complete, and everything is freedom.

Let's say we have a glass of water. Now its

temperature is about 60 degrees. If you reduce the temperature to 20 degrees, it becomes ice. If you raise the temperature above 212 degrees, it will become steam. As the temperature changes, H_2O in the form of water appears and disappears, but H_2O does not appear and does not disappear. Ice, water, and steam are only its form. Name and form change, but H_2O does not change. If you understand the temperature, then you understand the form. Your true self is like this.

But what is your true self? Your body has life and death. But your true self has no life, no death. You think, "My body is me." This is not correct. This is crazy. You must wake up!

Steam, ice, and water are all H_2O; but if you are attached to water, and the water becomes ice, then you say the water disappeared. So it is dead! Raise the temperature; the water is born again! Raise the temperature again; the water disappears and becomes steam, and the water is again dead!

On the Zen Circle this is the area from 0 degrees to 90 degrees. If you are attached to something and it disappears, you suffer. If you are attached to only doing what you like, you suffer. Don't be attached to water, OK? Being attached to water is being attached to name and form. Name and form are always changing, changing, changing, nonstop. So name and form are emptiness. Another way to say this is that form is emptiness, emptiness is form. This understanding is 90 degrees on the Zen Circle.

But name and form are made by thinking. Water does not say, "I am water." Steam does not say, "I am steam." If you cut off all thinking, are you and the water the same or different? Same and different are made by your thinking. How can you answer? There is no form, no emptiness—no words. Attaining this is 180 degrees on the Zen Circle. If you open your mouth, you have already made a mistake.

If you cut off all thinking, you will see everything just as it is. Without thinking, water is water; ice is ice; steam is steam. No ideas hinder you. Then your correct relationship to H_2O in any form appears by itself. We call this "just-like-this." This is 360 degrees on the Zen Circle. Just-like-this mind is clear mind. Clear mind has no I-my-me. Without I-my-me you can perceive your correct relationship to H_2O and use it freely without desire for yourself. You will not suffer when water disappears and becomes ice or steam.

Your father's original face has no death and no life. His body appears and disappears but his Dharma body does not appear and does not disappear. You must recognize that all things are in your own mind. Just this is finding your true self. Great love, great compassion, and the great bodhisattva way come from this attainment. But don't simply believe my speech. You must actually attain this.

I hope you go only straight—don't know, try, try, try, soon find your father's original face, get enlightenment, and save all beings from suffering

Yours in the Dharma,

S.S.

LETTER 06
IT'S SO CURIOUS
Colette to Marguerite Moreno
10 April 1923

Born to Jules-Joseph Colette and Adèle-Eugenie Sidonie in Burgundy in 1873, Sidonie-Gabrielle Colette – known simply as Colette to her many fans – was a leading French writer responsible for dozens of bestselling novels and short stories, and, as a journalist, numerous essays and articles. She also lectured, wrote plays, danced and acted. In 1948, she was nominated for the Nobel Prize in Literature. In 1912, her mother, Sido, died of cancer. Just as Sido had refused to wear mourning clothes following the death of Colette's father, so too did Colette when her mother passed away. She also chose not to attend her funeral. But for many years she continued to grieve. Eleven years after the death of her mother, Colette wrote this letter to French actress Marguerite Moreno.

THE LETTER

Paris, April 10, 1923

Hello, my dear creature,
As I think you will get this letter in the morning,
how did you sleep, and for how long?

I've just come back and can't shake the memory
of your departure from this house, from which you
left shrouded and crying like an exile.

Guess what, I arrived home – to lunch on my
own – and I opened the drawer of my little desk to
get some money – and a single letter fell out: it
was a letter from my mother, one of her last,
written in pencil with unfinished words and
already suffused with her departure.

How strange: one can successfully resist tears
and "hold" oneself very well in the hardest hours.
But then, someone makes a friendly gesture behind
a window, one notices a blossom which was just a
bud yesterday, – or a letter slips from a drawer –
and everything falls apart.

I'll pick up some green paper for you this
afternoon. How good you were, how kind. I
admire you, I'm so used to the feeling. See you
soon. You're coming the day after tomorrow? Will I
see you? I kiss you from the bottom of my heart.

Don't forget me amongst your friends, they are equally mine because they love you, and I'm only jealous of the good they do for you.

Your

Colette

LETTER 07
A MAN IS NOT COMPLETELY BORN UNTIL HE BE DEAD
Benjamin Franklin to Elizabeth Hubbart
22 February 1756

Benjamn Franklin was many things in addition to being a Founding Father of the United States of America: activist, inventor, author, printer, businessman, diplomat, humorist, musician and scientist. He was also one of sixteen children fathered by Josiah Franklin. On 30 January 1756, one of Franklin's older brothers – John, a candlemaker and later a postmaster – died aged sixty-seven. Upon hearing the news, Franklin wrote a letter of condolence to Elizabeth Hubbart, John's grieving stepdaughter.

THE LETTER

Philadelphia, February 22, 1756

Dear Child

I condole with you, we have lost a most dear and
valuable relation, but it is the will of God and
Nature that these mortal bodies be laid aside, when
the soul is to enter into real life; 'tis rather an
embrio state, a preparation for living; a man is not
completely born until he be dead: Why then should
we grieve that a new child is born among the
immortals? A new member added to their happy
society? We are spirits. That bodies should be lent
us, while they can afford us pleasure, assist us in
acquiring knowledge, or doing good to our fellow
creatures, is a kind and benevolent act of God—
when they become unfit for these purposes and
afford us pain instead of pleasure—instead of an
aid, become an incumbrance and answer none of
the intentions for which they were given, it is
equally kind and benevolent that a way is provided
by which we may get rid of them. Death is that
way. We ourselves prudently choose a partial death.
In some cases a mangled painful limb, which
cannot be restored, we willingly cut off. He who
plucks out a tooth, parts with it freely since the

pain goes with it, and he that quits the whole body, parts at once with all pains and possibilities of pains and diseases it was liable to, or capable of making him suffer.

Our friend and we are invited abroad on a party of pleasure—that is to last for ever. His chair was first ready and he is gone before us. We could not all conveniently start together, and why should you and I be grieved at this, since we are soon to follow, and we know where to find him.

Adieu,

B. F.

WHAT A WORLD
Ken Kesey to his friends
3 February 1984

One icy morning in January of 1984, as the University of Oregon's wrestling team headed on a bus to their next tournament in Pullman, Washington, the driver lost control of the vehicle on a mountain road and it tumbled through the guardrail and over a 300-foot cliff. Tragically, not all survived. One boy, Lorenzo West, was killed on impact; another, twenty-year-old Jed Kesey, was left brain dead. He passed away within days. Shortly after Jed's funeral at his family's farm, his father, One Flew Over the Cuckoo's Nest *author Ken Kesey, wrote to five of his closest friends.*

THE LETTER

Pleasant Hill, OR
February 3, 1984

Dear Wendell and Larry and Ed and Bob and
Gurnie:

Aw, partners, it's been a bitch.

I've got to write and tell somebody about some
stuff and, like I long ago told Larry, you're the best
backboard I know. So indulge me a little; I am but
hurt. [. . .]

We built the box ourselves (George Walker,
mainly) and dug the hole in a nice spot between
the chicken house and the pond (Zane and Jed's
friends, actually). Page found the stone and we
designed the etching. You would have been proud,
Wendell, especially of the box—clear pine pegged
together and trimmed with redwood. The handles
of thick hemp rope. And you, Ed, would have
appreciated the lining. It was a piece of Tibetan
brocade given Mountain Girl by Owsley fifteen
years ago, gilt and silver and russet phoenixbird
patterns, unfurling in flames. And last month, Bob,
Zane was goose hunting in the field across the road
and, just like I did years ago after Faye and I were
fresh wed, thought he saw a snow goose and

mistakenly killed a swan. I told him get it out of sight fast but be sure to pluck and save the down. Susan Butkovitch covered this in satin for the pillow while Faye and MG and Gretch and Candace stitched and stapled the brocade into the box.

It was a double-pretty day. Still is, like winter holding its breath for a week, giving us a break. About 300 people stood around and sung from the little hymnbooks that Diane Kesey had Xeroxed — Everlasting Arms, Sweet Hour of Prayer, In the Garden and so forth. With all my cousins leading the singing and Dale on his fiddle. While we were singing Blue Eyes Crying in the Rain, Zane and Kit and the neighbor boys that have grown up with all of us carried the box to the hole. The preacher is also the Pleasant Hill School superintendent and has known our kids since kindergarten. I learned a lot about Jed that I'd either forgotten or never known—like his being a member of the National Honor Society and finishing sixth in a class of more than a hundred.

We sung some more. People filed by and dropped stuff in on Jed. I put in that silver whistle I used to wear with the Hopi cross soldered on it. Somebody put in a quartz watch guaranteed to keep beeping every fifteen minutes for five years. Faye put in a snapshot of her and I standing with a pitchfork all Grantwoodesque in front of the bus. Paul Foster put in the little leatherbound New Testament given him by his father who had carried it during his sixty-five years as a minister. Paul Sawyer read from <u>Leaves of Grass</u> while the boys each hammered in the one nail they had remembered to put in their pockets. The Betas formed a circle and passed the Loving Cup Around (a ritual our fraternity generally uses when a member is leaving the circle to become engaged) (Jed and Zane and I are all members, y'unnerstand, not to mention Hagen) and the boys lowered the box with these ropes George had cut and braided. Zane and I tossed in the first shovelfuls. Good God, it sounded like the first thunderclaps of Revelations [. . .]

But it's an earlier scene I want to describe for you all, as writers and friends and fathers . . . up at the hospital, in cold awful Spokane:

He's finally started moving a little. Zane and I had been carrying plastic bags of snow to pack his head in trying to stop the swelling that all the doctors told us would follow as blood poured to the bruised brain. And we noticed some reaction to the cold. And the snow I brushed across his lips to ease the bloody parch where all the tubes ran in caused him to roll his arms a little. Then more.

Then too much, with the little monitor lights bleeping faster and faster, and I ran to the phone to call the motel where I had just sent most of the family for some rest, Faye included.

"You guys better get back over here. He's either going or coming."

Everybody was there in less than ten minutes—Chuck and Sue, Kit and Zane, Shan and her fiancé Jay, Jay's dad Irby, Sheryl and her husband Bill, Faye, my Mom . . . my whole family except for my dead daddy and Grandma Smith down with age and Alzheimer's. Jed's leg was shaking with the force of his heartbeat. Kit and Zane tried to hold it. He was about to go into seizures.

Up till this time everybody had been exhorting him to "hang on, Old Timer. Stick it out. This thing can't pin you. You're too tough, too brave. Sure it hurts but you can pull through it. Just grit your teeth and hang on." Now we could see him trying, fighting. We could see it in his clenching fists and threshing legs, and then aw Jesus we saw it in his face. The peacefully swollen unconscious blank suddenly was filled with expression. He came back in for a few seconds, and checked it out, and saw better than we could begin to imagine how terribly hurt he was. His poor face grimaced with pain. His purple brow knitted and his teeth actually did try to clench on the tubes.

And then, o my old buddies, he cried. The doctors had already told us in every gentle way they could that he was brain dead, gone for good, but we all saw it . . . the awful hurt, the tears saying "I don't think I can do 'er this time, Dad. I'm sorry, I truly am . . ."

And everybody said, "It's okay, ol' Jedderdink. Breathe easy. Go ahead on. We'll catch you later down the line."

His threshing stopped. His face went blank again. I thought of Old Jack, Wendell, ungripping his hands, letting his fields finally go.

The phone rang in the nurses' quarters. It was the doctor, for me. He had just appraised all the latest readouts on the monitors. "Your son is essentially dead, Mr. Kesey. I'm very sorry."

I said something. Zane picked up the extension and we watched each other while the voice explained the phenomena. We said we understood, and were not surprised. Thank you. Then the doctor asked a strange thing. He wanted to know what kind of kid Jed was. Zane and I both demanded what he meant. He said he was wondering how Jed would have felt about being an organ donor. Our hearts both jumped.

"He would love it! Jed's always been as generous as they come. Take whatever you can use!"

The doctor waited for our elation to ease down, then told us that to take the kidneys they had to take them before the life support was turned off. Did we understand? After a while we told him we did.

So Faye and I had to sign five copies apiece, on a cold formica countertop, while the machine pumped out the little "beep . . . beep . . . beep . . ." in the dim tangle of technology behind us. In all my life, waking and dreaming, I've never imagined anything harder.

Everybody went in and told him goodby[e], shook his hand, squeezed his big old hairy foot . . . headed down the corridor. Somebody said it might be a good idea to get a scrip for some kind of downers. We'd all been up for about forty hours, either in the chapel praying like maniacs, or at his bedside talking to him. We didn't know if we could sleep.

Chuck and I walked back to the Intensive Care ward to ask and all the doctors were there, bent over a long list, phoning numbers, matching blood types, ordering nurses . . . in such a hurry they barely noticed us.

They phoned the hotel about an hour later to

tell us it was over, and that the kidneys were in
perfect shape. That was about four A.M. They
phoned again a little after six to say that the
kidneys were already in two young somebodies.

What a world.

We've heard since that they used twelve things
out of him, including corneas. And the redwinged
blackbirds sing in the budding greengage plumtree.

With love,

Ken

PS: Looking to see if Wendell's name is spelled with
two l's and one e and two r's or one l and two e's
etc . . . I pull a book out of the shelf and it opens
to this:

> To go in the dark with a light is to know
>   the light.
> To know the dark, go dark. Go without sight,
>   and find that the dark, too, blooms and sings,
>   and is travelled by dark feet and dark wings.

LETTER 9
I LOVED HER SO MUCH
Audre Lorde to Martha Dunham
22 January 1990

*American poet and activist Pat Parker was born in
Houston in 1944. Her early life was marked by the
challenges and trauma caused by poverty, then later
she survived an abusive first husband, a miscarriage
and the murder of her sister, Shirley – all of which
informed her poetry. Parker died of breast cancer on
19 June 1989, aged forty-five. She was survived by her
partner, Martha 'Marty' Dunham, and her two
daughters, Cassidy and Anastasia. This letter reached
Dunham seven months later, written by Parker's
regular correspondent and fellow poet, the civil-rights
activist Audre Lorde, from her storm-ravaged home on
the island of Saint Croix. By sad coincidence, Lorde
also died of breast cancer, in 1992.*

THE LETTER

Dear dear Marty,

I am so happy to hear from you! I've been
wondering so often in these past terrible months
how you and Stasia are, and what's happening!

[Hurricane] Hugo was devastating, but we're
getting back on our feet—exuberantly came back
12/17—3 months to the day after, & we are
getting our roof put on right now & the glass
finally replaced, and expect the phones by
March. Gloria's fine, and I'm doing pretty well—
have started infusion treatments here again
because there are two new tumors in my liver, but
the old ones are shrunk and I am confident I
can beat it again. But if not, I'm living the life I
choose.

I can't tell you Marty what it means to me to
have the necklace from Pat—the reality of its power
& that she thought of me. I loved her so much,
Marty, and I feel her with me smiling so often. I
asked my mom & her & Gloria's mom to help us,
that terrible 13 hrs while Hugo mashed up our
island & we cowered in a corner listening to the
house breaking up around us. (And they did, too!)
We're alive!

Sweetheart, I am so happy you are moving on with your life. I know that doesn't mean you don't still mourn Pat sometimes, but the best memorial to someone we love who is gone is to live fully and richly with whatever that person gave us! I know that to the depth of my being, and I want you to know it too, because Patty would have wanted the best for you & Stasia. She loved you both, deeply, and when I promised her I would be whatever you needed me to be after she was gone (in our last telephone conversation) I meant it. Whatever.

If Kathleen is a good person and is good for you and Stasia, Pat would smile and bless you both and I sure do too. And don't you even listen for a moment to any meanness to the contrary!

You are a good woman, Marty, and I know what you gave Patty and how much you loved her, and also how very hard it sometimes was! And you deserve everything good out of life you ever find, for your devotion and your loyalty & your strength! There! I said it & I'm glad!

You tell Kathleen she's running with the Best, and hug Stasia for me. Tell her I'm coming out there again one of these days & we're gonna make some more house together!

Marty, sweetie, please remember I'm always here

for you, not to intrude but to support, however
you may need me.

Stay sweet!

Love Audre

P.S. Send me a photo of you and Stasia

St Croix
1-22-90

LETTER 10
MAKE IT YOUR AMBITION TO TAKE HEART
Rainer Maria Rilke to Sidonie Nádherná von Borutín
1 August 1913

By the time of his death from leukaemia in 1926, cele-
brated Austrian poet Rainer Maria Rilke had written
upwards of 14,000 letters, ten of which, famously, were
posthumously published in the collection Letters to a
Young Poet. *In 1906, Rilke met and formed a strong*
friendship with Sidonie Nádherná von Borutín, the host
of a literary salon. They corresponded often, and in
1913, following the suicide of her brother, Johannes
Nádherný von Borutín, Sidonie wrote to Rilke for
advice. This was his reply.

THE LETTER

August 1st, 1913
Currently Baltic Sea Spa, Heiligendamm,
Mecklenburg Grand Hôtel

My dear Sidie,

Your letter really touches my heart. On the one
hand, I want to encourage you in your pain so that
you will completely experience it in all its fullness,
because as the experience of a new intensity it is a
great life experience and leads everything back again
to life, like everything that reaches a certain degree
of greatest strength. But on the other hand, I am
very concerned when I imagine how strangled and
cut off you currently live, afraid of touching
anything that is filled with memories (and what is
not filled with memories?). You will freeze in place
if you remain this way. You must not, dear. You
have to move. You have to return to his things. You
have to touch with your hands his things, which
through their manifold relations and affinity are
after all also yours. You must, Sidie (this is the task
that this incomprehensible fate imposes upon you),
you must continue his life inside of yours insofar as it
was unfinished; his life has now passed onto yours.
You, who quite truly knew him, can quite truly

43

continue in his spirit and on his path. Make it the task of your mourning to explore what he had expected of you, had hoped for you, had wished to happen to you. If I could just convince you, my dear friend, that his influence has not vanished from your existence (how much more reliably I feel my father to be effective and helpful in me since he no longer dwells among us). Just think how much in our daily lives misleads and troubles us, and renders another person's love imprecise for us. But now he is definitely here, now he is completely free to be here and we are completely free to feel him . . . Haven't you felt your father's influence and compassion a thousand times from the universe where all, truly all, Sidie, is beyond loss? Don't believe that something that belongs to our pure realities could drop away and simply cease. Whatever had such steady influence on us had already been a reality independent of all the circumstances familiar to us here. This is precisely why we experienced it as something so different and independent of an actual need: Because from the very beginning, it had no longer been aimed at and determined by our existence here. All of our true relationships, all of our enduring experiences touch upon and pass through *everything*, Sidie, through life and death. *We must live in both, be intimately at home in both.* I know individuals who already face the one and the other without fear and with the same love—for is life really more demystified and safely entrusted to us than that other condition? Are not both conditions in a place namelessly beyond us, out of reach? We are true and pure only in our willingness to the whole, the undecided, the great, the greatest. Alas, if I could tell you just *how* I know it, then deep within your mourning, a tiny kernel of dark joy would take shape. Make it your ambition to take heart. Start doing so this very evening by playing Beethoven; he also was committed to the whole.

Yours,
Rainer

Please give my very best to Charlie.

I WILL BE THERE IN THE TREES

Kathleen Keyes to the *Irish Times*
December 2019

*As Christmas approached in December of 2019, with no
plans to celebrate the day, an Irish lady named
Kathleen Keyes, from Bray in County Wicklow, wrote a
beautiful letter to the* Irish Times *that would soon be
reprinted and shared across the land. In it, she spoke
of the difficulties posed by Christmas due to a tragic
chain of events that began in 2002, with the death of
her fifteen-year-old daughter, Gráinne, continued with
the death of her nineteen-year-old son, Darragh, in
2012, and ended with the death of her last child,
Fergal, in 2018. All had lived with cystic fibrosis.*

THE LETTER

Sir, – At this time of year, families are dreaming of seeing their loved ones. The loved ones coming back by sea, or touching down on tarmac, flowing through the arrivals lounge of airports, warm-cheeked and teary-eyed, breaking the barrier to the warm homely arms of childhood. Or coming by car, snapping the car doors shut for a while and walking in the front door of old familiarity – the family home. This is miracle-making.

Eighteen years ago this Christmas, my first child of three, my daughter was very ill and she died early in the New Year. It was a meteorite falling on a family that was already rocked by loss and absence. Since then, our family has been cruelly pared back to one, myself, the mother, living alone at home.

At night I sleep to the rattles of an empty house. Even the wind has a faraway cry when it rattles at the window. My three children, my daughter and two sons died from Cystic Fibrosis, a genetic disease of the lungs. They lived a full and spirited life together, their illness did not define them. They were witty, intelligent and gifted with homegrown talents that filled this home with music and liveliness. They expressed their true selves to their world of friends, and gave of themselves freely and honestly.

Losing a child is like having your heart torn out and your stomach emptied. Grief gets in the way of daylight, not to mention the nocturnal dark.

Christmas is a black surround, without tinsel, while the masses are plumping up the shopping streets.

But grief can be another day on the wheel, when paradoxically a blue sky can unveil and a white egret appears in the branch. I have named him Doy after my youngest son, whose pet name was Doy. He will fly and land with me as I walk beside the river in the valley behind our home.

Before Doy died, his dark eyes looked ahead and he said, "Look for me in the trees. I will be there in the trees." – Yours, etc,

KATHLEEN KEYES,
Bray, Co. Wicklow.

'LOSING A CHILD IS LIKE
HAVING YOUR HEART
TORN OUT AND YOUR
STOMACH EMPTIED.'

— Kathleen Keyes

LETTER 12
YOU MUST LET ME CRY MY CRY FOR HIM
Robert Frost to Helen Thomas
27 April 1917

*Born in 1878 in Lambeth, English war poet Edward
Thomas was thirty-seven when he joined the British
Army. He signed up after reading an advance copy of
The Road Not Taken, a poem written by his friend
Robert Frost, the only poet to receive four Pulitzer
Prizes. Thomas was killed in action during the Battle of
Arras on Easter Monday, 9 April 1917. He was survived
by his wife, Helen, and their three children. A few
weeks after Thomas died, Helen received this letter
from Frost, who was overcome with grief.*

THE LETTER

27 April 1917
Amherst

Dear Helen

People have been praised for self-possession in danger. I have heard Edward doubt if he was as brave as the bravest. But who was ever so completely himself right up to the verge of destruction, so sure of his thought, so sure of his word? He was the bravest and best and dearest man you and I have ever known. I knew from the moment when I first met him at his unhappiest that he would some day clear his mind and save his life. I have had four wonderful years with him. I know he has done this all for you: he is all yours. But you must let me cry my cry for him as if he were almost all mine too.

Of the three ways out of here, by death where there is no choice, by death where there is a noble choice, and by death where there is a choice not so noble, he found the greatest way. There is no regret—nothing that I will call a regret. Only I can't help wishing he could have saved his life without so wholly losing it and come back from France not too much hurt to enjoy our pride in

him. I want to see him to tell him something. I
want to tell him, what I think he liked to hear
from me, that he was a poet. I want to tell him
that I love those he loved and hate those he hated.
(But the hating will wait: there will be a time for
hate.) I had meant to talk endlessly with him still,
either here in our mountains as we had said or, as
I found my longing was more and more, there at
Leddington where we first talked of war.

It was beautiful as he did it. And I don't suppose
there is anything for us to do to show our admira-
tion but to love him forever.

Robert

LETTER 13
HOW COULD YOU GO AHEAD OF ME?
A widow to Eung-Tae Lee
1586

In 1998, shortly after excavating an ancient tomb in Andong City, South Korea, archaeologists were stunned to find the coffin of Eung-Tae Lee – a sixteenth-century male, now mummified, who had been a member of the country's ancient Goseong Yi clan. Resting on his chest was this letter, written by his pregnant widow and addressed to him as the father of their unborn child. Also found in the tomb, placed beside his head, were some sandals, woven from hemp bark and his distraught wife's own hair. The letter and tomb's discovery generated enormous interest in Korea, and the story has since been retold in novels, films and even operas. A statue of Eung-Tae Lee's pregnant wife now stands near his grave.

THE LETTER

To Won's Father

June 1, 1586

You always said, "Dear, let's live together until our hair turns gray and die on the same day." How could you pass away without me? Who should I and our little boy listen to and how should we live? How could you go ahead of me?

How did you bring your heart to me and how did I bring my heart to you? Whenever we lay down together you always told me, "Dear, do other people cherish and love each other like we do? Are they really like us?" How could you leave all that behind and go ahead of me?

I just cannot live without you. I just want to go to you. Please take me to where you are. My feelings toward you I cannot forget in this world and my sorrow knows no limit. Where would I put my heart in now and how can I live with the child missing you?

Please look at this letter and tell me in detail in my dreams. Because I want to listen to your saying in detail in my dreams I write this letter and put it in. Look closely and talk to me.

When I give birth to the child in me, who

should it call father? Can anyone fathom how I feel? There is no tragedy like this under the sky.

You are just in another place, and not in such a deep grief as I am. There is no limit and end to my sorrows that I write roughly. Please look closely at this letter and come to me in my dreams and show yourself in detail and tell me. I believe I can see you in my dreams. Come to me secretly and show yourself. There is no limit to what I want to say and I stop here.

LETTER 14
IT WAS SUPPOSED TO BE ME

An unknown soldier believed to have been
Basil Rathbone to Edgar Rathbone
26 July 1918

Basil Rathbone was forty-six years of age when he first donned the cap and pipe to become Sherlock Holmes in The Hound of the Baskervilles, *the first of thirteen movies to feature his iconic portrayal. Despite a long and illustrious career on stage and screen, it would be the Sherlock role that defined the South African-born actor. Decades earlier, Rathbone was called up to serve in the British Army during World War I. In July of 1918, while fighting on the Western Front, he received news that his younger brother and fellow soldier, John, had been killed in action. The next month, he wrote a letter to his father.*

THE LETTER

July 26th
Wed. morning

Dear father – We came up from the reserves a while ago, and just before we left I had your letter and also the parcel from uncle H. Please thank uncle and all the family especially the girls for their dear little poems. The whisky has already proved helpful. I shared the cake with my men and it was consumed in three minutes and pronounced to be pretty fair, which is high praise.

I'm sorry for the awful handwriting but it's very cold and I'm shivering terribly and there's only an inch of candle left in the dugout to write by and it flickers. It's 3.50 ack emma, so bitterly cold I'm wearing my great coat though it's July, but it's been a quiet night, and when I was out I caught a nice moon, very bright between little bits of cloud. I think it will be a very bright and sweet and warm day again like yesterday. Cloudless and a little breeze. Just the day for cricket.

Today will be quite a busy one and so I want to send this before it gets going.

I have all of Johnny's letters parcelled up together and I will either bring them home on my next leave or arrange for someone to deliver them in person. I would send them as you asked but I would be afraid of them being lost. The communication trenches can take a beating and nothing can be relied on. If I can't bring them myself for any reason there is a good sort here, another Lieutenant in our company who is under oath to deliver them, and who I have never known to shirk or break his word. So, you will get them, come what may.

I'm sorry not to have written much the past weeks. It was unfair and you are very kind not to be angry. You ask how I have been since we heard, well, if I am honest with you, and I may as well be, I have been seething. I was so certain it would be me first of either of us. I'm even sure it was supposed to be me and he somehow contrived in his wretched Johnny-fashion to get in my way just as he always would when he was small. I want to tell him to mind his place. I think of his ridiculous belief that everything would always be well, his ever-hopeful smile, and I want to cuff him for a little fool. He had no business to let it happen and it maddens me that I shall never be able to tell him so, or change it or bring him back. I can't think of him without being consumed with anger at him for being dead and beyond anything I can do to him.

I'm afraid it's not what you hoped for from me and perhaps that's why I haven't written. I suspect you want me to say some sweet things about him. I wish I could for your sake, but I don't have them to say. Out here we step over death every day. We stand next to it while we drink our tea. It's commonplace and ordinary. People who had lives and tried to hold on to them and didn't, and now slump and stare and melt slowly to nothing. You meet their eyes, or what used to be their eyes and you feel ashamed. And now Johnny is one of them. That's an end of it. Grieving is only ridiculous in this place. It could be me today or tomorrow and I shouldn't want anyone to bother grieving over that.

Stand to is being called. I have to go now. God bless you and Bea. You are both dearer to me than I could ever say. Take very good care of each other won't you.

With my best love
PSB

THE MISTS OF GRIEF
Helen Keller to Takeo and Keo Iwahashi
27 July 1950

Helen Keller was born in Alabama in 1880. Before she reached the age of two, she lost her sight and hearing. In the face of this challenging start to life, she went on to do incredible things: by the age of twenty-three, her autobiography was published; over the years she travelled the world as a highly sought-after public speaker, giving eloquent lectures on all manner of topics, including her inspiring life story; and all told, she authored a dozen books. As an activist, she campaigned tirelessly on behalf of the marginalised. In 1937, she was invited to Japan by Takeo Iwahashi, the founder of the Nippon Lighthouse for the Blind, who wanted to know if she could help promote his centre. She did exactly that, and they became firm friends. In 1950, Keller was informed that his daughter, Edina, had died. Keller wrote this letter to Takeo and his wife, Keo, in response.

THE LETTER

Arcan Ridge, July 27, 1950

Dear Takeo and Keo,

Words cannot tell you how shocked and grieved
Polly and I were at the cruel manner in which
sweet Edina had been taken from you. For us who
remember Edina's bright face, her affectionate,
charming ways and her enthusiasm in helping the
blind such a fate seems incredible.

There is nothing I can say, dear friends, to touch
a sacred sorrow like yours. Too well do I know
from my own experience that much time will pass
before the mists of grief lift from your minds, and
you can see that God has permitted your loss for
His mysterious Purpose of Good. But I do not
forget the vivid sense that some of the Buddhists
have of the nearness of their loved ones in death.
So much more will you rejoice in the radiant
beauty of Edina's new life as she comes back to
you in memory and the gentle inspiration of her
earthly endeavors. It is Teacher's [Annie Sullivan,
Keller's lifelong teacher, who died in 1936]
spiritual nearness that has strengthened me to carry
on my work alone a second time in the silent dark,
except for Polly's devoted ministrations.

It moves me to the verge of tears that you should have remembered my birthday in the midst of your sadness. It was a blessed day for me — I spent it quietly in Paris — and I received greetings from all parts of the world, but your loving thought touched me in a peculiar way, and I thank you from my heart.

You give me welcome news about the arrival in Nippon of the rubber products from Brooklyn and the materials and instruments from the American Foundation for the Blind. I hope the books too will reach you before long.

Yes, I shall be happy to write a message for Mr. Sakata's translation of "The Education of Exceptional Children." It is splendid that Mr. Sakata and other leading teachers of Japan are responding to the challenge to fit the handicapped as far as possible for useful, normal lives.

Polly and I send you both and Hideyuki our love and the fervent prayer that you may all be comforted. We shall cherish Edina's picture and yours too in our home.

Devotedly your friend,
Helen Keller

'THERE IS NOTHING I
CAN SAY, DEAR FRIENDS,
TO TOUCH A SACRED
SORROW LIKE YOURS.'

— Helen Keller

LETTER 16
WHAT IS IT THAT YOU MOURN IN A FRIEND'S DEATH?

Marsilio Ficino to Bernardo Bembo

c. 1472

Marsilio Ficino was an Italian scholar and priest of enormous stature who, as head of the Platonic Academy in Florence, led a group of fifteenth-century philosophers who regularly met to discuss and translate the works and philosophy of Plato and others. Ficino also found the time to write thousands of letters to correspondents across Europe, from family and friends through to fellow philosophers and even, on occasion, the Pope. One acquaintance to whom he wrote often was statesman and ambassador of Venice Bernardo Bembo. It was around 1472 that this letter was penned, following the death of a friend of Bembo.

THE LETTER

Tell me, Bernardo, what is it that you mourn in a friend's death? Is it death? Or is it the person who is dead? If it is death, mourn your own, Bernardo. For as surely as he is dead will you too die; or rather, you are dying; for from moment to moment your past life is dying. If it is the dead person you mourn, is it because he was bad, or because he was good? If he was bad, you are well rid of such a companion; and you should not grieve over your blessings. If he was good, which I prefer to think since he is loved by a good and prudent man, surely for him it is good to live removed from the continuous death of the body. It is not right to grudge a friend such great blessings. Perhaps you grieve because you no longer see him anywhere as you used to. However, was not this man your friend in that he loved you? Now what was it that loved you? Was it not the soul itself, the soul which also knew you? But you saw his soul no differently then than now; and you see it now no less than then.

You will perhaps complain of his absence. But, as souls do not fill space, they become present not in any particular place but in thought. When you do not consider him you cannot be sad. But when you do consider him, which you do as you please, you at once recall his presence. You should never complain about his absence then, unless perhaps you object that it is not the way of the free soul to commune with the one now imprisoned in your body. Separate the mind from the body, Bernardo, if you can, and, believe me, your souls will quickly meet. But if you cannot do this, do not doubt they will meet a little later whether you will or no. For if we compare our life to our will, it is exceedingly brief; if we compare it to the age of the world, it is but an instant; and, compared to the age of God, even less than an instant.

Farewell, and live in God, since He alone is eternal life. He alone drives death and the sorrow of death far from His worshippers.

LETTER 17
THE HEAVY HAND OF DEATH
Kahlil Gibran to Mary Haskell
23 June 1909

Celebrated poet Kahlil Gibran was born in 1883 in the Lebanese city of Bsharri, to Khalil Sa'd Jubran and Kamila Rahmeh. Twelve years later, his mother took him and his siblings to the US in search of a better life away from their absent father, settling first in Boston and later in New York. In 1902, tragedy struck when Gibran's younger sister died from tuberculosis, then in March of the next year his brother, Boutros, died of the same disease. Life took yet another dark turn three months later when Gibran's mother, Kamila, died of cancer, leaving him to grieve with his remaining sister Marianne. In 1909, as he studied art in Paris, Gibran received word that his estranged father had also died and he wrote to his friend and patron, Mary Haskell, with the news.

THE LETTER

June 23, 1909
Paris

Dear Mary—

I have lost my father, beloved Mary. He died in the old house where he was born sixty-five years ago. His last two letters make me weep bitterly each time I read them. His friends wrote saying that he blessed me before the end came. I know now, dear Mary, that he rests in the bosom of God; and yet I cannot help but feel the pains of sorrow and regret. I cannot help but feel the heavy hand of Death on my forehead. I cannot help but see the dim, sad shadows of the bygone days when he and my mother and my brother and my young sister lived and smiled before the face of the sun. Where are they now? Are they somewhere in an unknown region? Are they together? Do they remember the past as we do? Are they near this world of ours or are they far faraway? I know, dear Mary, that they live. They live a life more real, more beautiful than ours. They are nearer to God than we are.

The veil of seven folds is no longer hanging between their eyes and Truth. They no longer play hide and seek with the Spirit. I feel all this beloved Mary and yet I cannot help but feel the pains of sorrow and regret.

And you—you dear sweet consolation, you are now in Hawaii—in the islands so much loved by the sun. You are on the other side of this planet. Your days are nights in Paris. You belong to another order of time. And yet you are so near me. You walk with me when I am alone; you sit across the table in the evening and you talk to me when I am working. There are times when I feel as though you are not here on earth.

I am taking notes of the different works of modern artists like Rodin and Carrière and Henry Martin and Simon and Ménard. Each has something to say and says it in a different way. The work of Carrière is the nearest to my heart. His figures, sitting or standing behind the mist, say more to me than anything else except the work of Leonardo da Vinci. Carrière understood faces and hands more than any other painter. He knew the depths, the height, and the width of the human figure. And Carrière's life is not less beautiful than his work. He suffered much, but he understood the mystery of pain: he knew that tears make all things shine.

Remember me to the valleys and mountains of Hawaii.

I kiss your hand, dear Mary, I close my eyes now and I see you, beloved friend.

Kahlil

LETTER 18
HOW ARE YOU FEELING?
Jessica Mitford to Eva and Bill Maas
22 August 1993

*David Jenkins, leader of the California Labor School,
died in June 1993. He was survived by his wife, Edith.
Two months after his death, Edith attended a party
hosted by Eva and Bill Mass, and spent the whole
evening in the company of mutual friend Jessica
Mitford, the famous English author and a sixth of the
Mitford sisters. This letter of thanks, written by
Mitford to Eva Mass, arrived soon after.*

THE LETTER

Dearest Eva & Bill,

Thanks SO much for inviting us to yr absolutely
spiffing party. It was like being a drowning man, &
seeing everyone one's ever known swim before
one's eyes . . .

I must tell a wee vignette before I forget it all.
Edith Jenkins arrived same time I did, so we sat
together. She started telling me about a big gathering (I forget what for) that she went to a few
days ago—her first real social outing since David
died, so she was much looking forward to it.

Person after person came up to her with
variations on the theme of "How are you feeling,
my dear?" "It must have been a terrible blow." "Are
you all right?" "Are you over the worst of it?" and
much more along same lines. Edith said that by the
end of the evening, she felt as though she'd had
open heart surgery—which I thought was rather
apt & clever. So the entire time was ruined.

So there are Edith & I sitting together, & just
after she'd related this, somebody came up to
where we were & said to Edith "How are you

feeling? It must have been such a terrible blow. I do hope you are over the worst of it . . ." literally, the exact words of the Edith gathering from several days before. Needless to say I was overcome with giggles & gave E. a sharp pinch in the behind. After that, she stayed by my side upon my promise to protect her from future well-wishers. (I can't remember the first person—nobody I know; but lots more DID come up with similar mournful dirges, but I fended them off with "so sorry, Edith & I were just telling a few jokes.")

The crème de la crème was Barb. Kahn, who came up & said how sorry she was that David died and she had meant to write a letter, but was awfully busy. After she left, Edith said that next time anyone says that she'll say "As you were too busy to write, please shut up!"

However, as E. & I were giggling through it all, it turned out rather well & I think she really did enormously enjoy the party . . . I'm planning to write to Miss Manners to ask her opinion of correct behaviour on these occasions.

Again—trillion thanks for smashing lunch.

Fondest love, Decca

LETTER 19
NO ONE YOU LOVE IS EVER DEAD
Ernest Hemingway to Gerald and Sara Murphy

19 March 1935

Gerald and Sara Murphy married in 1916, and in 1921 moved from New York City to France – living first in Paris, then in the French Riviera. It was there they had three children – Baoth, Patrick and Honoria – and befriended many of literature's 'Lost Generation', a collective of American novelists living in France, which included Gertrude Stein, F. Scott Fitzgerald and Ernest Hemingway. In 1935, some years after leaving France due to their son Patrick's ill-health, their other son, Baoth, died of meningitis. This letter, from Hemingway, soon reached them. Tragically, two years later, their grief intensified with the death of Patrick.

THE LETTER

Dear Sara and Dear Gerald:

You know there is nothing we can ever say or
write. If Bumby died we know how you would feel
and there would be nothing you could say. Dos and
I came in from the Gulf Sunday, and sent a wire.
Yesterday I tried to write you and I couldn't.

It is not as bad for Baoth because he had a fine
time, always, and he has only done something now
that we all must do. He has just gotten it over with.
It was terrible that it had to go on for such a long
time but if they could keep him from suffering
sometimes it is merciful to get very tired before
you die when you want to live very much.

About him having to die so young—Remember
that he had a very fine time and having it a
thousand times makes it no better. And he is spared
from learning what sort of a place the world is.

It is *your* loss: more than it is his, so it is
something that you can, legitimately, be brave
about. But I can't be brave about it and in all my
heart I am sick for you both.

Absolutely truly and coldly in the head, though,

I know that anyone who dies young after a happy childhood, and no one ever made a happier childhood than you made for your children, has won a great victory. We all have to look forward to death by defeat, our bodies gone, our world destroyed; but it is the same dying we must do, while he has gotten it all over with, his world all intact and the death only by accident.

You see now we have all come to the part of our lives where we start to lose people of our own age. Baoth was our own age: very few people ever really are alive and those that are never die; no matter if they are gone. No one you love is ever dead.

We must live it, now, a day at a time and be very careful not to hurt each other. It seems as though we were all on a boat now together, a good boat still, that we have made but that we know now will never reach port. There will be all kinds of weather, good and bad, and especially because we know now that there will be no landfall we must keep the boat up very well and be very good to each other. We are fortunate we have good people on the boat.

With all our love to you both and to the Duke of Taxidermy [son Patrick Murphy] and to Honoria [daughter] of the Horses and to old Baoth.

Ernest

LETTER 20
LET ME BEG OF YOU NOT TO INDULGE IN USELESS GRIEF

Lady Mary Wortley Montagu to Mary Stuart,
Countess of Bute
20 August 1752

Lady Mary Wortley Montagu was born in the English hamlet of Holme Pierrepont in 1689 to Evelyn and Mary Pierrepont. She was a noblewoman famous, in part, for The Turkish Embassy Letters *(1763), a travel memoir inspired by her voyage to Turkey with her husband, Edward Wortley Montagu, who for two years worked as the British ambassador to the Ottoman Empire. It was there, in January of 1718, that they had a daughter, Mary, who in 1736 married the prime minister of the United Kingdom, John Stuart, 3rd Earl of Bute. In 1752, Lady Montagu wrote to Mary, who at the time was grieving the loss of a friend.*

THE LETTER

Louvere, August 20, 1752

MY DEAR CHILD,

'Tis impossible to tell you to what degree I share
with you in the misfortune that has happened. I
do not doubt your own reason will suggest to
you all the alleviations that can serve on so sad an
occasion, and will not trouble you with the
common-place topics that are used, generally to no
purpose, in letters of consolation. Disappointments
ought to be less sensibly felt at my age than yours;
yet I own I am so far affected by this, that I have
need of all my philosophy to support it. However,
let me beg of you not to indulge [in] useless
grief, to the prejudice of your health, which is so
necessary to your family. Every thing may turn out
better than you expect. We see so darkly into
futurity, we never know when we have real cause
to rejoice or lament. The worst appearances have
often happy consequences, as the best lead many
times into the greatest misfortunes. Human
prudence is very straitly bounded. What is most in
our power, though little so, is the disposition of
our own minds. Do not give way to melancholy,
seek amusements; be willing to be diverted, and

insensibly you will become so. Weak people only place a merit in affliction. A grateful remembrance, and whatever honour we can pay to their memory, is all that is owing to the dead. Tears and sorrow are no duties to them, and make us incapable of those we owe to the living.

I give you thanks for your care of my books. I yet retain, and carefully cherish, my taste for reading. If relays of eyes were to be hired like post-horses, I would never admit any but silent companions: they afford a constant variety of entertainment, and is almost the only one pleasing in the enjoyment, and inoffensive in the consequence. I am sorry your sight will not permit you a great use of it: the prattle of your little ones, and friendship of Lord Bute, will supply the place of it. My dear child, endeavour to raise your spirits, and believe this advice comes from the tenderness of your most affectionate mother,

M. WORTLEY

LETTER 21
THE EVERLASTING NEST

'Abdu'l-Bahá to bereaved parents

Date unknown

'Abdu'l-Bahá was head of the Bahá'í Faith from 1892 until his death thirty years later, having taken over from his father, Bahá'u'lláh, the founder of the religion. It is the firm belief of Bahá'ís that the human soul exists beyond the death of a human body, and in fact blossoms and gains strength as it makes its eternal journey towards perfection. For this reason, they say, death is not to be feared. This belief was expanded upon in a letter written by 'Abdu'l-Bahá to two grieving parents.

THE LETTER

O ye two patient souls! Your letter was received.
The death of that beloved youth and his separation
from you have caused the utmost sorrow and
grief; for he winged his flight in the flower of his
age and the bloom of his youth to the heavenly
nest. But he hath been freed from this sorrow-
stricken shelter and hath turned his face toward
the everlasting nest of the Kingdom, and, being
delivered from a dark and narrow world, hath
hastened to the sanctified realm of light; therein
lieth the consolation of our hearts.

The inscrutable divine wisdom underlieth such
heart-rending occurrences. It is as if a kind
gardener transferreth a fresh and tender shrub from
a confined place to a wide open area. This transfer
is not the cause of the withering, the lessening or
the destruction of that shrub; nay, on the contrary,
it maketh it to grow and thrive, acquire freshness
and delicacy, become green and bear fruit. This
hidden secret is well known to the gardener, but
those souls who are unaware of this bounty
suppose that the gardener, in his anger and wrath,
hath uprooted the shrub. Yet to those who are
aware, this concealed fact is manifest, and this
predestined decree is considered a bounty. Do not

feel grieved or disconsolate, therefore, at the ascension of that bird of faithfulness; nay, under all circumstances pray for that youth, supplicating for him forgiveness and the elevation of his station.

I hope that ye will attain the utmost patience, composure and resignation, and I entreat and implore at the Threshold of Oneness, begging for forgiveness and pardon. My hope from the infinite bounties of God is that He may shelter this dove of the garden of faith, and cause him to abide on the branch of the Supreme Concourse, that he may sing in the best of melodies the praise and glorification of the Lord of Names and Attributes.

LETTER 22
HOW IT SEIZES UPON ONE
Virginia Woolf to Dora Carrington
2 March 1932

*For much of his adult life, English writer Lytton
Strachey lived at Ham Spray House with fellow author
and beloved companion Dora Carrington, their
years-long bond both platonic and passionate. When
he died on 21 January 1932 of stomach cancer,
Carrington's world fell apart. Almost two months after
Strachey's death, Carrington received this letter from
friend and fellow Bloomsbury writer Virginia Woolf,
who was also, it seems, in the throes of grief for the
loss of Lytton. A week later, on 10 March, sensing the
depth of her heartbreak, Woolf paid a brief visit to
Carrington in an effort to console her. The next day,
on 11 March, unable to continue on without Strachey,
Carrington took her own life.*

THE LETTER

I loved those little pictures, darling Carrington.
How it seizes upon one, the longing for Lytton,
when one sees them. But then how happy he looks
– that is one comfort – and then again I thank you.
We would always have come to Ham Spray: it was
only the feeling we had that that belonged to
another side of Lytton's life: I dont mean that you
didn't want us, but that it was simpler for him to
come here. But heavens – how I wish we had
brushed aside all that, and come and stayed: or
made him come here oftener. Of course one gets
involved in things, and there is always the press,
and Leonards different things – how worthless it
seems now compared with one hour of being with
Lytton. Yes, I think it does get harder – I cant
describe to you the sense I have of wanting to tell
Lytton something. I never read a book even with
the same pleasure now. He was part of all I did – I
have dream after dream about him and the oddest
sense of seeing him coming in the street.

Oh but Carrington we have to live and be
ourselves – and I feel it is more for you to live

than for any one; because he loved you so, and loved your oddities and the way you have of being yourself. I cant explain it; but it seems to me that as long as you are there, something we loved in Lytton, something of the best part of his life still goes on. But goodness knows, blind as I am, I know all day long, whatever I'm doing, what you're suffering. And no one can help you. [. . .]

Goodbye, darling Carrington
your old attached friend
Virginia

LETTER 23
YOU WILL NOT HAVE MY HATRED
Antoine Leiris to his wife's killers
November 2015

On the evening of 13 November 2015, the lives of 130
people were cut short, and those of hundreds more
irrevocably changed, when a wave of coordinated
terrorist attacks brought unimaginable pain to the
bustling city of Paris and its suburb, Saint-Denis.
Eighty-nine of those deaths were lost at the Bataclan
theatre, where gunmen opened fire indiscriminately
within its walls as a jubilant audience danced and sang
along to a live rock band. One of those eighty-nine
was thirty-five-year-old Hélène Muyal, a make-up artist
and music lover who was survived by her husband,
Antoine, and their seventeen-month-old son. Soon after
the attack tore his family apart, Antoine wrote an
open letter to his wife's killers.

THE LETTER

On Friday evening you stole the life of an exceptional person, the love of my life, the mother of my son, but you will not have my hatred.

I don't know who you are and I don't want to know, you are dead souls. If this God for whom you kill blindly made us in his image, every bullet in the body of my wife is a wound in his heart.

So no, I will not give you the satisfaction of hating you. You want it, but to respond to hatred with anger would be to give in to the same ignorance that made you what you are.

You would like me to be scared, for me to look at my fellow citizens with a suspicious eye, for me to sacrifice my liberty for my security. You have lost.

I saw her this morning. At last, after nights and days of waiting. She was as beautiful as when she left on Friday evening, as beautiful as when I fell head over heels in love with her more than 12 years ago.

Of course I am devastated with grief, I grant you this small victory, but it will be short-lived. I know she will be with us every day and we will find each other in heaven with free souls which you will never have.

Us two, my son and I, we will be stronger than every army in the world. I cannot waste any more time on you as I must go back to my son who has just woken from his sleep. He is only just 17 months old. He is going to eat his snack just like every other day, then we are going to play like every other day and all his life this little boy will be happy and free. Because you will never have his hatred either.

Antoine Leiris

LETTER 24
FOR SHE WAS MORTAL BORN
Servius Sulpicius Rufus and Marcus Tullius Cicero
March 45 BC

Born in 75 BC, Tullia was the only daughter of Marcus Tullius Cicero, the Roman philosopher and politician thought to have been the greatest orator in the history of Rome. In February of 45 BC, tragedy struck when Tullia died from complications related to the birth of her second son. Her death haunted her father for the rest of his life. Many letters reached Cicero as he mourned his daughter, including, in March, a message from friend and noted jurist Servius Sulpicius Rufus. Cicero responded the next month.

THE LETTERS

When I received the news of your daughter Tullia's death, I was indeed as much grieved and distressed as I was bound to be, and looked upon it as a calamity in which I shared. For, if I had been at home, I should not have failed to be at your side, and should have made my sorrow plain to you face to face. That kind of consolation involves much distress and pain, because the relations and friends, whose part it is to offer it, are themselves overcome by an equal sorrow. They cannot attempt it without many tears, so that they seem to require consolation themselves rather than to be able to afford it to others. Still I have decided to set down briefly for your benefit such thoughts as have occurred to my mind, not because I suppose them to be unknown to you, but because your sorrow may perhaps hinder you from being so keenly alive to them.

Why is it that a private grief should agitate you so deeply? Think how fortune has hitherto dealt with us. Reflect that we have had snatched from us what ought to be no less dear to human beings than their children—country, honour, rank, every political distinction. What additional wound to your feelings could be inflicted by this particular loss?

Or where is the heart that should not by this time have lost all sensibility and learn to regard everything else as of minor importance? Is it on her account, pray, that you sorrow? How many times have you recurred to the thought—and I have often been struck with the same idea—that in times like these theirs is far from being the worst fate to whom it has been granted to exchange life for a painless death? Now what was there at such an epoch that could greatly tempt her to live? What scope, what hope, what heart's Solace? That she might spend her life with some young and distinguished husband? How impossible for a man of your rank to select from the present generation of young men a son-in-law, to whose honour you might think yourself safe in trusting your child! Was it that she might bear children to cheer her with the sight of their vigorous youth? who might by their own character maintain the position handed down to them by their parent, might be expected to stand for the offices in their order, might exercise their freedom in supporting their friends? What single one of these prospects has not been taken away before it was given? But, it will be said, after all it is an evil to lose one's children. Yes, it is: only it is a worse one to endure and submit to the present state of things.

I wish to mention to you a circumstance which gave me no common consolation, on the chance of its also proving capable of diminishing your sorrow. On my voyage from Asia, as I was sailing from Aegina towards Megara, I began to survey the localities that were on every side of me. Behind me was Aegina, in front Megara, on my right Piraeus, on my left Corinth: towns which at one time were most flourishing, but now lay before my eyes in ruin and decay. I began to reflect to myself thus: "Hah! do we mannikins feel rebellious if one of us perishes or is killed—we whose life ought to be still shorter—when the corpses of so many towns lie in helpless ruin? Will you please, Servius, restrain yourself and recollect that you are born a mortal man?" Believe me, I was no little strengthened by that reflexion. Now take the trouble, if you agree with me, to put this thought before your eyes. Not long ago all those most illustrious men perished at one blow: the empire of the Roman people suffered that huge loss: all the provinces were shaken to their foundations. If you have become the poorer by the frail spirit of one poor girl, are you agitated thus violently? If she had not died now, she would yet have had to die a few years hence, for she was mortal born. You, too, withdraw soul and thought from such things, and rather remember those which become the part you have played in life: that she lived as long as life had anything to give her; that her life outlasted that of the Republic; that she lived to see you—her own father-praetor, consul, and augur; that she married young men of the highest rank; that she had enjoyed nearly, every possible blessing; that, when the Republic fell, she departed from life. What fault have you or she to find with fortune on this score? In fine, do not forget that you are Cicero, and a man accustomed to instruct and advise others; and do not imitate bad physicians, who in the diseases of others profess to understand the art of healing, but are unable to prescribe for themselves. Rather suggest to yourself and bring home to your own mind the very maxims which you are accustomed to impress upon others. There is no sorrow beyond the power of time at length to diminish and soften: it is a reflexion on you that you should wait for this period, and not rather anticipate that result by the aid of your wisdom. But if there is any consciousness still existing in the world below, such was her love for you and her dutiful affection for all her family, that she certainly does not wish you to act as you are acting. Grant this to her—your lost one! Grant it to your friends and comrades who mourn with you in your sorrow! Grant it to your country, that if the need arises she may have the use of your services and advice.

Finally—since we are reduced by fortune to the necessity of taking precautions on this point also—do not allow anyone to think that you are not mourning so much for your daughter as for the state of public affairs and the victory of others. I am ashamed to say any more to you on this subject, lest I should appear to distrust your wisdom. Therefore I will only make one suggestion before bringing my letter to an end. We have seen you on many occasions bear good fortune with a noble dignity which greatly enhanced your fame: now is the time for you to convince us that you are able to bear bad fortune equally well, and that it does not appear to you to be a heavier burden than you ought to think it. I would not have this be the only one of all the virtues that you do not possess.

As far as I am concerned, when I learn that your mind is more composed, I will write you an account of what is going on here, and of the condition of the province.

Good-bye.

* * *

YES, indeed, my dear Servius, I would have wished—as you say—that you had been by my side at the time of my grievous loss. How much help your presence might have given me, both by consolation and by your taking an almost equal share in my sorrow, I can easily gather from the fact that after reading your letter I experienced a great feeling of relief. For not only was what you wrote calculated to soothe a mourner, but in offering me consolation you manifested no slight sorrow of heart yourself. Yet, after all, your son Servius by all the kindnesses of which such a time admitted made it evident, both how much he personally valued me, and how gratifying to you he thought such affection for me would be. His kind offices have of course often been pleasanter to me, yet never more acceptable. For myself again, it is not only your words and (I had almost said) your partnership in my sorrow that consoles me, it is your character also. For I think it a disgrace that I should not bear my loss as you—a man of such wisdom—think it should be borne. But at times I am taken by surprise and scarcely offer any resistance to my grief, because those consolations fail me, which were not wanting in a similar misfortune to those others, whose examples I put before my eyes. For instance, Quintus Maximus, who lost a son who had been consul and was of illustrious character and brilliant achievements, and Lucius Paullus, who lost two within seven days, and your kinsman Gallus and M. Cato, who each lost a son of the highest character and valour;—all lived in circumstances which permitted their own great position, earned by their public services, to assuage their grief. In my case, after losing the honours which you yourself mention, and which I had gained by the greatest possible exertions, there was only that one solace left which has now been torn away. My sad musings were not interrupted by the business of my friends, nor by the management of public affairs: there was nothing I cared to do in the forum: I could not bear the sight of the senate-house; I thought—as was the fact—that I had lost all the fruits both of my industry and of fortune. But while I thought that I shared these losses with you and certain others, and while I was conquering my feelings and forcing myself to bear them with patience, I had a refuge, one bosom where I could find repose, one in whose conversation and sweetness I could lay aside all anxieties and sorrows. But now, after such a crushing blow as this, the wounds which seemed to have healed break out afresh. For there is no republic now to offer me a refuge and a consolation by its good fortunes when I leave my home in sorrow, as there once was a home to receive me when I returned saddened by the state of public affairs. Hence I absent myself both from home and forum, because home can no longer console the sorrow which public affairs cause me, nor public affairs that which I suffer at home. All the more I look forward to your coming, and long to see you as soon as possible. No reasoning can give me greater solace than a renewal of our intercourse and conversation. However, I hope your arrival is approaching, for that is what I am told. For myself, while I have many reasons for wishing to see you as soon as possible, there is this one especially—that we may discuss beforehand on what principles we should live through this period of entire submission to the will of one man who is at once wise and liberal, far, as I think I perceive, from being hostile to me, and very friendly to you. But though that is so, yet it is a matter for serious thought what plans, I, don't say of action, but of passing a quiet life by his leave and kindness, we should adopt.

Good-bye.

LETTER 25
LIKE A TREE IN FULL BEARING STRUCK AT THE ROOT
Charlotte Brontë to W.S. Williams
25 December 1848

Charlotte Brontë was the eldest of the Brontë sisters, three creative English siblings born in the nineteenth century whose most successful novels, all of which were published in the space of nine months, are now considered classics: Charlotte's Jane Eyre, *Emily's* Wuthering Heights *and Anne's* The Tenant of Wildfell Hall. *They are arguably the most famous of all literary families. In 1848, a year after the publication of her aforementioned magnum opus, Emily, the middle sister, died from tuberculosis; she was just thirty years old. A few days later, Charlotte wrote to her publisher.*

THE LETTER

Decb 25th 1848

My dear Sir,

I will write to you more at length when my heart
can find a little rest – now I can only thank you
very briefly for your letter, which seemed to me
eloquent in its sincerity.

Emily is nowhere here now, her wasted mortal
remains are taken out of the house. We have laid
her cherished head under the church aisle beside
my mother's, my two sisters' – dead long ago –
and my poor, hapless brother's. But a small remnant
of the race is left – so my poor father thinks.

Well, the loss is ours, not hers, and some sad
comfort I take, as I hear the wind blow and feel the
cutting keenness of the frost, in knowing that the
elements bring her no more suffering; their severity
cannot reach her grave; her fever is quieted, her
restlessness soothed, her deep, hollow cough is
hushed for ever; we do not hear it in the night nor
listen for it in the morning; we have not the
conflict of the strangely strong spirit and the fragile
frame before us—relentless conflict—once seen,
never to be forgotten. A dreary calm reigns round
us, in the midst of which we seek resignation.

My father and my sister Anne are far from well. As for me, God has hitherto most graciously sustained me; so far I have felt adequate to bear my own burden and even to offer a little help to others. I am not ill; I can get through daily duties, and do something towards keeping hope and energy alive in our mourning household. My father says to me almost hourly, "Charlotte, you must bear up, I shall sink if you fail me"; these words, you can conceive, are a stimulus to nature. The sight, too, of my sister Anne's very still but deep sorrow wakens in me such fear for her that I dare not falter. Somebody must cheer the rest.

So I will not now ask why Emily was torn from us in the fulness of our attachment, rooted up in the prime of her own days, in the promise of her powers; why her existence now lies like a field of green corn trodden down, like a tree in full bearing struck at the root. I will only say, sweet is rest after labour and calm after tempest, and repeat again and again that Emily knows that now.

Yours sincerely,

C. Brontë

'SOME SAD COMFORT I
TAKE, AS I HEAR THE
WIND BLOW AND FEEL
THE CUTTING KEENNESS
OF THE FROST, IN
KNOWING THAT THE
ELEMENTS BRING HER
NO MORE SUFFERING.'

— Charlotte Brontë

LETTER 26
THE SPRINGTIME SUN BRINGS FORTH NEW LIFE

Albert Einstein to Queen Elisabeth of Belgium
20 March 1936

*Duchess Elisabeth in Bavaria was born in 1876. In 1909
she became Queen Elisabeth of Belgium when her
husband, Prince Albert, ascended to the Belgian throne
after his uncle's death. Fifteen years later, Elisabeth's
life darkened when Albert, a keen climber, died as he
attempted to scale a cliff in Marche-les-Dames. He was
fifty-eight. The next year, darkness descended once
again when Elisabeth's daughter-in-law, Astrid of
Sweden, was killed when the car in which she and
Elisabeth's son, King Leopold III, were travelling crashed
into a tree as they holidayed in Switzerland. Months
later, as she struggled to come to terms with these
tragedies, Elisabeth received a letter of support from
her friend, Albert Einstein.*

THE LETTER

Dear Queen,

Today, for the first time this year, the spring sunshine has made its appearance, and it aroused me from the dreamlike trance into which people like myself fall when immersed in scientific work. Thoughts rise up from an earlier and more colorful life, and with them comes remembrance of beautiful hours in Brussels.

Mrs. Barjansky wrote to me how gravely living in itself causes you suffering and how numbed you are by the indescribably painful blows that have befallen you.

And yet we should not grieve for those who have gone from us in the primes of their lives after happy and fruitful years of activity, and who have been privileged to accomplish in full measure their task in life.

Something there is that can refresh and revivify older people: joy in the activities of the younger generation—a joy, to be sure, that is clouded by dark forebodings in these unsettled times. And yet, as always, the springtime sun brings forth new life, and we may rejoice because of this new life and contribute to its unfolding; and Mozart remains as beautiful and tender as he always was and always will be. There is, after all, something eternal that lies beyond reach of the hand of fate and of all human delusions. And such eternals lie closer to an older person than to a younger one oscillating between fear and hope. For us, there remains the privilege of experiencing beauty and truth in their purest forms.

Have you ever read the Maxims of La Rochefoucauld? They seem quite acerbic and gloomy, but by their objectivization of human and all-too-human nature they bring a strange feeling of liberation. In La Rochefoucauld we see a man who succeeded in liberating himself even though it had not been easy for him to be rid of the heavy burden of the passions that Nature had dealt him for his passage through life. It would be nicest to read him with people whose little boat had gone through many storms: for example, the good Barjanskys. I would gladly join in were it not forbidden by "the big water."

I am privileged by fate to live here in Princeton as if on an island that in many respects resembles the charming palace garden in Laeken. Into this small university town, too, the chaotic voices of human strife barely penetrate. I am almost ashamed to be living in such peace while all the rest struggle and suffer. But after all, it is still the best to concern oneself with eternals, for from them alone flows that spirit that can restore peace and serenity to the world of humans.

With my heartfelt hope that spring will bring quiet joy to you also, and will stimulate you to activity, I send you my best wishes.

AE

LETTER 27
WE FEEL DOUBLY BEREFT
Ethel Bedsow to Jacqueline Kennedy
c. 1964

On 22 November 1963, as an open-top motorcade took him and the First Lady through Dealey Plaza in downtown Dallas, the 35th President of the United States, John F. Kennedy, was assassinated by a sniper situated in a nearby building. The shock was global and profound, and within two months of Kennedy's death his widow, Jacqueline, had received almost a million letters of condolence from members of the public. This particular letter came from a lady who grieved not just for the loss of the president but also for the loss of Jacqueline and her two children, who were now, understandably, slipping from public view.

THE LETTER

Chicago,
Illinois

My dear Mrs. Kennedy:

I just saw your lovely face on television and heard you speak. And all the while, a feeling of great pain overwhelmed me because I know that your public appearances will be all too few and the family we have come to love so dearly will become news we find occasionally in the papers. Yes, we have come to think of all of you as belonging to us. It was so wonderful to feel part of the great excitement our dear president gave us all. And to be part of you, watching the children grow and seeing the grace and beauty both of you brought to our land. Yes, a lovely bright light went out for us, and we share with you and the children and the family the tragic loss that can never become a thing of objectivity. But we have another loss—we have lost you and the children and we miss you very much. We felt that we could watch Caroline and John-John grow, and share with you and our beloved president the joy of family. And now we feel doubly bereft.

I know you have received so many messages

very much like this one, but I did want to tell you how lonely we are for the sight of our First Family. The brightness and electric excitement have gone out of the news, for we cannot get used to turning on the television and not seeing that wonderful smile and the brilliant eyes. We could tell when a wry remark was coming and watched for it in delighted anticipation. It isn't the same anymore. We will back everything he fought for so hard, because of him, but there is no pleasure behind it. I do not mean any disrespect to Mr. Johnson for I know how hard it must be for him to even begin to fill a role that such a brilliant, sparkling man left vacant. But ordinary men seem to be in government now. And government will go back to being ordinary once more.

Please don't disappear from our view. We want to know how you are faring, how the children are, if you all are well, and above all we want to have you lean back and rest against us, knowing that our love does sustain you and is there for you and the children, dear Mrs. Kennedy. We know how great was your loss because our loss was great too. How we love him; I shall not say loved, because his memory will not dim for us. He was a lovely shining knight and we are thankful that we were privileged to know him and to have him lead us.

May I write to you from time to time to find out if you are all right and if the children are all right too: We love you very much and don't want to lose touch. We hope to be able to come to Washington soon to visit "our grave" and pay our respects.

Keep well and God watch over you and the children.

With deepest affection,
Ethel Bedsow

LETTER 28
THE BUSINESS OF LIFE SUMMONS US
AWAY FROM USELESS GRIEF
Samuel Johnson to James Elphinston
25 September 1750

In 1746, English writer Samuel Johnson began work on
A Dictionary of the English Language, a book which,
when finally published nine years later, was considered
to be one of the most important dictionaries of its
time. Indeed, its influence is still felt today. It was in
the middle of that laborious process that he wrote this
letter to his dear friend James Elphinston, a master of
linguistics responsible for adapting Johnson's bi-weekly
periodical, The Rambler, for a Scottish audience, and
whose beloved mother had recently died.

THE LETTER

Friday, September 25, 1750

Dear Sir,

You have, as I find by every kind of evidence, lost an excellent mother; and I hope you will not think me incapable of partaking of your grief. I have a mother, now eighty-two years of age, whom, therefore, I must soon lose, unless it please God that she should rather mourn for me. I read the letters in which you relate your mother's death to Mrs. Strahan, and think I do myself honour, when I tell you, that I read them with tears; but tears are neither to you nor to me of any farther use, when once the tribute of nature has been paid. The business of life summons us away from useless grief, and calls us to the exercise of those virtues, of which we are lamenting our deprivation.

The greatest benefit which one friend can confer upon another, is to guard, and excite, and elevate his virtues. This your mother will still perform, if you diligently preserve the memory of her life, and of her death: a life, so far as I can learn, useful, wise, and innocent; and a death, resigned, peaceful, and holy. I cannot forbear to mention, that neither reason nor revelation denies you to hope that you may increase her happiness by obeying her precepts; and that she may, in her present state, look with pleasure upon every act of virtue to which her instructions or example have contributed. Whether this be more than a pleasing dream, or a just opinion of separate spirits, is, indeed, of no great importance to us, when we consider ourselves as acting under the eye of God: yet, surely, there is something pleasing in the belief, that our separation from those whom we love is merely corporeal; and it may be a great incitement to virtuous friendship, if it can be made probable, that that union, which has received the divine approbation, shall continue to eternity.

There is one expedient, by which you may, in some degree, continue her presence. If you write down minutely what you remember of her from your earliest years, you will read it with great pleasure, and receive from it many hints of soothing recollection, when time shall remove her yet farther from you, and your grief shall be matured to veneration. To this, however painful for the present, I cannot but advise you, as to a source of comfort and satisfaction in the time to come for all comfort and all satisfaction is sincerely wished you by, dear Sir.

Your most obliged, most obedient, and most humble servant,

Sam. Johnson

LETTER 29
SORROW COMES TO ALL
Abraham Lincoln to Fanny McCullough
23 December 1862

As the American Civil War raged in December of 1862, US President Abraham Lincoln received word that Lieutenant Colonel William McCullough, whom he had befriended many years before while working as a lawyer in Illinois, had recently been killed in battle. He left behind a distraught twenty-two-year-old daughter so suffocated by grief she was barely able to function. Her worrying refusal to eat and inability to sleep prompted a mutual friend, David Davis of the Supreme Court, to make Lincoln, who long ago had played with her as a child, aware of Fanny's deep depression. This compassionate letter was Lincoln's response.

THE LETTER

Executive Mansion,
Washington, December 23, 1862.

Dear Fanny

It is with deep grief that I learn of the death of your
kind and brave Father; and, especially, that it is
affecting your young heart beyond what is common
in such cases. In this sad world of ours, sorrow
comes to all; and, to the young, it comes with
bitterest agony, because it takes them unawares. The
older have learned to ever expect it. I am anxious to
afford some alleviation of your present distress.
Perfect relief is not possible, except with time. You
can not now realize that you will ever feel better. Is
not this so? And yet it is a mistake. You are sure to
be happy again. To know this, which is certainly
true, will make you some less miserable now. I have
had experience enough to know what I say; and you
need only to believe it, to feel better at once. The
memory of your dear Father, instead of an agony,
will yet be a sad sweet feeling in your heart, of a
purer and holier sort than you have known before.

Please present my kind regards to your afflicted
mother.

Your sincere friend

A. Lincoln

'SORROW COMES TO ALL; AND TO THE YOUNG, IT COMES WITH BITTEREST AGONY.'

— *Abraham Lincoln*

THE GREAT WALL

Thomas Wolfe and Marjorie Kinnan Rawlings to
Maxwell E. Perkins
1938

In July of 1938, American novelist Thomas Wolfe was struck down with pneumonia and taken to hospital. He was soon diagnosed as having tuberculosis of the brain, from which he would never recover. Wolfe died on 15 September, aged just thirty-seven. A month before his death, as he lay in hospital, Wolfe wrote to his old editor Maxwell Perkins, a once dear friend with whom he had fallen out in 1936 but still loved dearly. Days after Wolfe's death, Perkins received a letter from another of his authors, Marjorie Kinnan Rawlings, who was acutely aware of the sorrow he now felt, and to whom Perkins had shown Wolfe's final missive.

THE LETTERS

Providence Hospital
Seattle, Washington
August 12, 1938

Dear Max:

I'm sneaking this against orders, but "I've got a hunch"—and I wanted to write these words to you.

I've made a long voyage and been to a strange country, and I've seen the dark man very close; and I don't think I was too much afraid of him, but so much of mortality still clings to me—I wanted most desperately to live and still do, and I thought about you all a thousand times, and wanted to see you all again, and there was the impossible anguish and regret of all the work I had not done, of all the work I had to do—and I know now I'm just a grain of dust, and I feel as if a great window has been opened on life I did not know about before— and if I come through this, I hope to God I am a better man, and in some strange way I can't explain, I know I am a deeper and a wiser one. If I get on my feet and out of here, it will be months before I head back, but if I get on my feet, I'll come back.

Whatever happens—I had this "hunch" and wanted to write you and tell you, no matter what happens or has happened, I shall always think of you and feel about you the way it was that Fourth of July day three years ago when you met me at the boat, and we went out on the café on the river and had a drink and later went on top of the tall building, and all the strangeness and the glory and the power of life and of the city was below.

Yours always,

Tom

*   *   *

Hawthorne, Florida
September 21, 1938

Dear Max:

I have grieved for you ever since I heard of Tom's death. I grieve, too, for the certain loss of the work he would unquestionably have done, for his very touching letter to you shows a chastening and mellowing of that great half-mad diffusive ego, that would have been a guarantee of the literary self-discipline we all so wanted for him. It seems that each of us can go only so far in wisdom and in insight, and then for one reason or another we are done. And no one can take up where another leaves off. No one can profit by all that Tom had come to learn, with so much torture to himself and to others. Just as civilizations never learn from other civilizations, but must build up agonizingly, making the same mistakes over and over, with never any cumulative progress.

I know how glad you must be that you never withdrew your personal goodness from Tom, even when others were bitter for you.

It is strange that so vibrant and sentient a personality as Tom knew or guessed that he had come to the great wall. He must have felt far beyond most of us that withdrawing of the cosmic force from his individual unit of life. I felt the thing this summer for myself, knowing—and I still know—that if I had done the thing I planned I should not have come through. I felt the reprieve, too, and I am still puzzled. It is like the hurricane scheduled for the Florida coast the other day, that suddenly swerved from its path and swept on elsewhere. It is all accidental and incidental, and yet why is it so often one knows in advance?

I have thought of you a great deal since hearing, and I hope it is something you can accept without too much pain.

Marjorie

LETTER 31
NOW HER SOUL IS FREE
Ram Dass to Steve and Anita Isser
1979

One afternoon in the winter of 1979, the small village of Ashland, South Oregon, was forever changed when an eleven-year-old girl named Rachel was found murdered within walking distance of her home. Soon after the tragedy occurred, enveloped in grief, Rachel's parents received an unexpected, profound letter from a spiritual teacher named Ram Dass that gave them renewed strength.

THE LETTER

Dear Steve and Anita,

Rachel finished her work on earth, and left the
stage in a manner that leaves those of us left
behind with a cry of agony in our hearts, as the
fragile thread of our faith is dealt with so violently.
Is anyone strong enough to stay conscious through
such teaching as you are receiving? Probably very
few. And even they would only have a whisper of
equanimity and peace amidst the screaming
trumpets of their rage, grief, horror and desolation.

I can't assuage your pain with any words, nor
should I. For your pain is Rachel's legacy to you.
Not that she or I would inflict such pain by choice,
but there it is. And it must burn its purifying way
to completion. For something in you dies when
you bear the unbearable, and it is only in that dark
night of the soul that you are prepared to see as
God sees, and to love as God loves.

Now is the time to let your grief find expression. No false strength. Now is the time to sit
quietly and speak to Rachel, and thank her for
being with you these few years, and encourage her
to go on with whatever her work is, knowing that
you will grow in compassion and wisdom from
this experience. In my heart, I know that you and

she will meet again and again, and recognize the many ways in which you have known each other. And when you meet you will know, in a flash, what now it is not given to you to know: Why this had to be the way it was.

Our rational minds can never understand what has happened, but our hearts — if we can keep them open to God — will find their own intuitive way. Rachel came through you to do her work on earth, which includes her manner of death. Now her soul is free, and the love that you can share with her is invulnerable to the winds of changing time and space.

In that deep love,
include me.

In love,
Ram Dass

'FOR SOMETHING IN
YOU DIES WHEN YOU
BEAR THE UNBEARABLE,
AND IT IS ONLY IN
THAT DARK NIGHT OF
THE SOUL THAT YOU
ARE PREPARED TO SEE AS
GOD SEES, AND TO LOVE
AS GOD LOVES.'

— Ram Dass

PERMISSION CREDITS

LETTER 2 Nick Cave, letter 'Grief is non-negotiable' to Cynthia, October 2018, published in *The Red Hand Files*, Issue 6, Oct 2018, https://www.theredhandfiles.com/communication-dream-feeling/. Reproduced by permission of the author.

LETTER 3 Edith Wharton, letter 'A great desert lies ahead of me' to John Hugh Smith, October 15, 1927, from *The Letters of Edith Wharton*, 1989, Simon & Schuster. Reproduced by permission of the Estate of Edith Wharton and the Watkins/Loomis Agency.

LETTER 5 Zen Master Seung Sahn, letter 'Your true self has no life, no death' to Sheldon, August 18, 1977, from *Only Don't Know: Selected Teaching Letters of Zen Master Seung Sahn*, edited by Hyon Gak Sunim, copyright ©1982, 1999 by Providence Zen Center. Reproduced by arrangement with The Permissions Company, LLC on behalf of Shambhala Publications Inc., www.shambhala.com.

LETTER 6 Sidonie-Gabrielle Colette, letter 'It's so curious' to Marguerite Moreno, 10 April 1923, from *Lettres à Marguerite Moreno*, Flammarion, 1994, copyright © 1959. Translation reproduced by permission of the Estate of the author.

LETTER 8 Ken Kesey, letter 'What a world', 1984, copyright © Ken Kesey. Reproduced by permission of SLL/Sterling Lord Literistic, Inc.

LETTER 9 Audre Lorde, letter 'I loved her so much' to Marty Dunham, January 22, 1990, from *Sister Love: The Letters of Audre Lorde and Pat Parker 1974-1989* by Julie R. Enszer. Reproduced by permission of Abner Stein.

LETTER 10 Rainer Maria Rilke, letter 'Make it your ambition to take heart' to Sidonie Nádherná von Borutín, 1 August 1913 from *The Dark Interval: Letters on Loss, Grief and Transformation* by Rainer Maria Rilke, translated by Ulrich Baer, copyright © 2018 by Ulrich Baer. Used by permission of Modern Library, an imprint of Random House, a division of Penguin Random House LLC. All rights reserved.

LETTER 11 Kathleen Keyes, letter 'I will be there in the trees' published in *The Irish Times*, December 2019. Reproduced with kind permission from Kathleen Keyes.

LETTER 12 Robert Frost, letter 'You must let me cry my cry for him' to Helen Thomas, from *Selected Letters of Robert Frost*, ed Lawrance Thompson, copyright © 1964 by Lawrance Thompson and Holt, Rhinehart, and Winston, Inc. Reprinted by permission of Henry Holt and Company; and The Random House Group Limited. All Rights Reserved.

LETTER 15 Helen Keller, letter 'The Mists of Grief' to Takeo and Keo Iwahashi, July 27, 1950, https://www.afb.org/HelenKellerArchive?a=d&d=A-HK01-03-B062-F06-028&e=-------en-20--1--txt--------3-7-6-5-3--------------0-1. Copyright © American Foundation for the Blind, Helen Keller Archive.

LETTER 17 Kahlil Gibran, letter 'The heavy hand of death' to Mary Haskell, June 23, 1909, from *Beloved Prophet: The Love Letters of Kahlil Gibran and Mary Haskell, and Her Private Journal*, 1972, Penguin Random House USA Inc.

LETTER 18 Jessica Mitford, letter 'How are you feeling?' to Eva and Bill Maas, August 22, 1993, from *Decca: The Letters of Jessica Mitford*, ed Peter Y. Sussman, copyright © 2006 by Constancia Romilly and Benjamin Treuhaft, Editing and commentary copyright © 2006 by Peter Y. Sussman. Reproduced by permission of Hill Nadell Literary Agency.

LETTER 19 Ernest Hemingway, letter 'No one you love is ever dead' to Gerald and Sara Murphy, March 19, 1935, from *Ernest Hemingway, Selected Letters 1917-1961* by Carlos Baker, editor, copyright © 1981 by Carlos Baker and The Ernest Hemingway Foundation, Inc. Reproduced with the permission of Scribner, a division of Simon & Schuster, Inc. All rights reserved.

LETTER 21 Abdu'l-Bahá, letter '169: O ye two patient souls! Your letter was received. . . .' published in *The Writings of 'Abdu'l-Bahá*, https://reference.bahai.org/en/t/ab/SAB/sab-170.html, Bahá'í World Centre, 1988.

LETTER 22 Virginia Woolf, letter 'How it Seizes Upon One' to Dora Carrington, 2 March 1932, from *Congenial Spirits: The Selected Letters of Virginia Woolf*. Letter copyright © 1979 by Quentin Bell and Angelica Garnett. Reproduced by permission of The Society of Authors; and Houghton Mifflin Harcourt Publishing Company; and The Random House Group Limited. All rights reserved.

LETTER 25 Charlotte Bronte, letter 'Like a tree in full bearing' to W. S. Williams, 25 December 1848. Original source: British Library, Ashley MS 2452, https://www.bl.uk/collection-items/

ACKNOWLEDGEMENTS

It requires a dedicated team of incredibly patient people to bring the Letters of Note books to life, and this page serves as a heartfelt thank you to every single one of them, beginning with my wife, Karina — not just for her emotional support during such stressful times, but for the vital role she has played as Permissions Editor on many of the books in this series. Special mention, also, to my excellent editor at Canongate Books, Hannah Knowles, who has somehow managed to stay focused despite the problems I have continued to throw her way.

Equally sincere thanks to all of the following: Teddy Angert and Jake Liebers, whose research skills have helped make these volumes as strong as they are; Rachel Thorne and Sasmita Sinha for their crucial work on the permissions front; the one and only Jamie Byng, whose vision and enthusiasm for this series has proven invaluable; all at Canongate Books, including but not limited to Rafi Romaya, Kate Gibb, Vicki Rutherford and Leila Cruickshank; my dear family at Letters Live: Jamie, Adam Ackland, Benedict Cumberbatch, Aimie Sullivan, Amelia Richards, and Nick Allott; my agent, Caroline Michel, and everyone else at Peters, Fraser & Dunlop; the many illustrators who have worked on the beautiful covers in this series; the talented performers who have lent their stunning voices not just to Letters Live, but also to the Letters of Note audiobooks; Patti Pirooz; every single archivist and librarian in the world; everyone at Unbound; the team at the Wylie Agency for their assistance and understanding; my foreign publishers for their continued support; and, crucially, my family, for putting up with me during this process.

Finally, and most importantly, thank you to all of the letter writers whose words feature in these books.

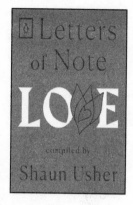 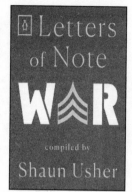